Swallowed by
ALS Tsunami

SWALLOWED BY
ALS TSUNAMI

AUTOBIOGRAPHY: ANVERALI NAJAK

ALS—Amyotrophic Lateral Sclerosis or Lou Gehrig's disease

ISBN: 978-1-4669-0993-9 (sc)
ISBN: 978-1-4669-0992-2 (e)

Trafford rev. 01/03/2011

 www.trafford.com

North America & International
toll-free: 1 888 232 4444 (USA & Canada)
phone: 250 383 6864 ♦ fax: 812 355 4082

In the end, what will matter is every act of integrity, compassion, or sacrifice that enriched, empowered, or encouraged others to emulate my example

My last word to my family and friends

First of all, I would like to thank my wife and my daughter Alysha for really taking care of me all these years, especially during the last few years of my sickness. I have lived a very happy life and have no regrets in life, the only one being I will not be able to teach Ayaan a lot of things which would help him to choose a good career in his life.

I would like to thank you for having the patience to bear with me and to type my words as I narrated them to you, I know it was very difficult often because I was talking to a mask, special thanks to Doug Wong, Alex Abraham and Madeleine Benoit the visiting Nurse.

Thanks to Sarah McGuire for constant help and guidance. ALS society for provided me with all the equipment to partly survive the tsunami attach of ALS.

Thanks to Josh Willms for correcting and proof reading the script, to Az, thank you for your guidance and creativity.

Thanks to my relatives and friends for visiting, uplifting me and bringing delicious foods.

The Good Old Days End

It was early in the morning, about 6:30am, and I was traveling along the skyway in Burlington, on my way to work in Hamilton, at US Steel. For a newcomer or tourist, the view from the skyway presents a beautiful scene. Excess gas from a blast furnace burns into a large, unabated plume, emitting bright light into the heaving, yet empty horizon. The coke ovens similarly release continuous smoke and carcinogens into the atmosphere. Nearby, thick clouds of steam rise from the central boiler station and other major leaks in the plant, spreading rapidly into the cold air and camouflaging the old, crumbling plant. Out on the water, hundreds of private boats race out of the harbor and into the lake, as if trying to escape the pollutants. As I observed this scene from the skyway, I wondered to myself, "How much longer am I going to work here?" Since the takeover of Stelco by the American-owned US Steel, my job was no longer a challenge; all of the research and innovation in the company took place in the United States. Retirement seemed to be the only option, I thought, but how can a creative, active, analytical man sit idle?

Just a couple of days earlier, my wife and I had bought a Laundromat in Etobicoke, at the intersection of Lakeshore Boulevard and Islington Avenue. It was similar to the Laundromat that I had owned in Hamilton twenty years earlier, but in better condition. "This small business would keep me on my toes," I thought. I would have to help my wife at the Laundromat in the evenings, and run the Laundromat on my own on weekends. I would be working long hours, but that is true with any business owner.

The motor neurons in my brain were acting normally, as was my spinal cord. I had full control of my muscles. I enjoyed learning how to repair my own machines, usually by reading and following the instructions in the manual. On weekends, I would go to the Laundromat early in the morning. Around eleven o'clock, I would go to the gym to have a nice work-out, and to relax in the steam room sauna. I would then re-energize myself with a good lunch before I returned to work, where I'd stay until about three o'clock in the afternoon. These were fun times; the business was booming.

I retired the following year, after thirty-one years of service. During retirement, I remained active in my personal life and in the community. I had a lot of fun playing tennis with Nabi; our games were usually very close and entertaining. I continued to run/walk five miles once a week near my house. My voluntary service on Fridays at the mosque also continued. I was in charge of special projects at the mosque, bringing together youths and seniors to impart knowledge and entertain them. Volunteering at the mosque often required a lot of creativity; for instance, I remember creating a Jeopardy-style quiz, with an electronic buzzer system, and researching questions for the quiz that covered current affairs, history, music, sports, and other subjects. I also used to travel with my volunteering team to other mosques in the Greater Toronto Area to deliver this program, which was always appreciated by the youths and seniors that we were visiting.

One hot, early Saturday morning, with the birds still sleeping in their nests, our neighbor's cats appeared outside the patio door near the kitchen, and stared inside the kitchen, looking, as if something unusual was going to happen. Our neighbor's dog, usually very quiet in the morning, started barking. All of a sudden, my daughter rushed into the house, and declared to my wife, "Mom, I am pregnant." There was jubilation and an aroma of happiness floating in the air. It appeared that my neighbor's pets already knew of the good news! While I celebrated, I said to my God, "What's going on? You're keeping me so happy! Now, one more wish. Give me a grandson."

Shortly after hearing the news of my daughter's pregnancy, Nabi, my tennis partner, called to ask if I was interested in playing tennis with him the following day. "Yes," I told Nabi. It was always a pleasure playing with him.

When Nabi played tennis the next day, on Sunday afternoon, I noticed something strange. Nabi was, surprisingly, returning my first serve with tremendous ease. This had never happened before. I was totally amazed. I tried to put more pressure and strength into my serve, but there was no change. "Is there something wrong with my racket?" I thought. Moreover, following only a half an hour of playing, I started to grow tired, which was very unusual for me.

My religion teaches me that there will be always ups and downs in life; you cannot have everything in life because, otherwise, you will cease to be a human being, and become like God. I had not seen a doctor in ten years, nor did I need to see a doctor during that time. However, following my tennis game with Nabi on that Sunday afternoon, just one day after the news of my daughter's pregnancy, I decided it was a good time to finally see my family doctor. My family doctor sent me for a complete blood test. My Vitamin B12 was low, so she *immediately* gave me a B12 injection. When the results of my blood test came in, the family Doctor called me, and . . . GUESS WHAT.

It's a Boy

As the sun set under the blue African sky in Kyere Teso District, a small village in central Uganda, east Africa, my mother held her sick child—my sister Zarina—to her chest. It was a quiet, humdrum evening; the only noise came from the birds that were returning to rest for the evening in their home, a nest in the sweet pear tree in our backyard.

"How many more girls am I going to have?" my mother, Shirin, contemplated. Zarina, my mother's third daughter, was tremendously sick, suffering from a severe bout of pneumonia; she had troubles breathing and a very high fever. The doctor in town had already given up hope. Zarina's two sisters hugged their mother as tears flowed from her eyes like an African river: "Can't anyone do something to cure my sick baby?"

As the skies grew dark, Zarina's condition deteriorated even further. Suddenly, at around ten o'clock in the evening, a loud cry erupted: "Oallah! Oallah!" My entire family screamed as the sick Zarina left this world.

The days following Zarina's burial were very tough. Many people in the village consoled my family, and often cried with them, too, which did help to alleviate their suffering after such a terrible loss. My family was very prominent in the village; we were liked by young and old, rich and poor. My father was a very kind, humble, smart and creative man. All of these attributes would make my father a very successful business man, and made our family renowned in the village. My father was in charge of the security of the entire village, leading the security vigilantes that looked after business properties and the general safety of the people in the community. My father was also in charge of the village well, where people would fetch water for drinking and other uses. He was always willing to help the indigenous local residents of the village, and used to celebrate Muslim holidays, such as Mohammad's birthday, by hosting a large feast for the entire village.

My father would often travel to Soroti, the nearest town from the family's village, to buy goods. He also used to visit his mother and brothers in Soroti whenever he went on these trips. For my mother, though, these trips were uncomfortable, because everyone would ask her when she was going to have a boy. Every day that passed seemed to put more pressure on my mother to finally have a boy; once, her mother-in-law—my grandmother—almost successfully brainwashed my father into casting out my mother from our family's house because she had not yet given birth to a boy.

Following Zarina's death, my father was very suspicious of trying to have another child; he said that whatever God wants to give us, He will give us. The women elders in the village, however, persuaded my mother to have another child. Eventually, my mother and two sisters were then able to convince my father to have another child.

My mother would ask the elders, "What about another girl?" But Rukyabai, a well-respected elder in the village, promised, if my mother took to her guidance, that her next child would be a boy. Rukyabai was a staunch believer, and practiced Ithna-asheri Islam—Ithna-asheri Muslims are commonly known as Twelvers—though she had actually been born into an Ismaili family. Rukyabai insisted that my mother change her faith from Ismaili. If she really wanted a son, but my mother refused. However, my mother did concede that, if her baby was a boy, she would take her son to the Ithana-asheri mosque, perform Salam on Imam Hussein during Muhharam, and participate in the Ashura ceremony every year. Rukyabai also convinced my mother that, in order to have a boy, she was required to wake up at four o'clock in the morning to pray and, for seven days, invite the young girls in the village for delicious foods and to pray together after the meal.

One hot evening, after Eid-ul-Fitre, my sister saw my mother vomiting and knew right away that my mother was pregnant. The news of my mother's pregnancy brought a smile in the face, song in the heart, and spring in the step of everyone in the family. The melancholies of the house suddenly disappeared, and were replaced by the revival of love and joy. However, my mother's pregnancy was very difficult; she experienced a lot of vomiting, stomach pains, bleeding, and loss of appetite. According to my mother, these symptoms were completely different from her previous three pregnancies. Nevertheless, the family's neighbors and friends in the village regularly visited my mother, and took her out of the house for fresh air and long walks. There was also more spiritualism in the house during my mother's pregnancy; my mom and sisters regularly recited the Koran, and incense burned twenty four hours a day. It is said angels witnessed the birth of Jesus Christ in the same, maybe some supernatural beings witnessed my birth in Soroti hospital.

There were a lot of celebrations and festivities at home to celebrate the birth of "the golden boy," as I was called. Villagers returning to our community from a party at the next village had heard about my birth and, on their way back home, stopped in front of our house to perform the GOMA dance, a local traditional African dance with sticks and colorful customs. Soon, the whole village had come out to this event, even blocking the road, for a time, during their celebration. I was given such a great welcome when I entered this world. At the same time, they were expecting a lot from me; after all, I was "the golden boy." Could I deliver on their expectations? If I didn't, it would always haunt me. My mother would try to have another boy, twice, but she gave birth to a girl both times. As a result, my parents ended up with four girls, and only one golden boy.

MY YOUTH

Following my birth, my mother was very insistent that we move to the town of Soroti. My father also believed that the family would have to move to town, for the benefit of the children's education. In Soroti, my father built our house, with two stores in the front of the building and residences in the back. Half of the house was rented out, and our family lived in the other half. Initially, the store was rented to a photographer, who opened a camera store. Meanwhile, my father worked as the manager of a hardware warehouse for G.R. Hansraj, who was from a rich Muslim family. The aim, however, was that, once we were settled, my father would open a Duka—a general purpose store—in the front of our house and call it DUKA YA HUSSEIN.

After working at the hardware warehouse for a couple of years, my dad finally opened a Duka at the front of our house, replacing the photographer's camera store. My father sold all of the necessities of the indigenous people in Soroti. People in town quickly came to know of my father's Duka, and business at the store flourished. My father was a very generous man, as he immediately started selling goods on credit at his store.

The mwalimu—the head teacher at the school across the road from our house—and Imam—the head priest at the mosque across the road from our house—as well as worshippers who went to the mosque, held my father in high regard, and always promoted his store.

As a young boy, I was accepted into the only government-run primary school in Soroti. At school, my life was completely different from the other five—and six-year old kids. Every minute of my time at school was constantly monitored by my mother and sisters. My parents chose my friends and activities for me. In fact, I was not allowed to go anywhere without my parents; after all, I was the golden boy of the family. On the other hand, I was allowed to have things that my parents didn't allow my sisters to have. For instance, I remember it being very expensive to buy apples and grapes. Due to government restrictions Uganda could not import apples and grapes grown in South Africa. Instead, these fruits had to be exported from South Africa to England, and then shipped to Uganda. Nobody could afford eating the sweet apples and grapes from South Africa, but my mother knew that I liked these fruits, so, whenever I became sick, she would buy them for me. Years later, when I began my job in Hamilton, only three days after I had moved to Canada, one of my co-workers would ask me what I was going to do during my first weekend in Canada. I'd reply to him that I was going to the market to eat apples and grapes for the entire weekend. He'd laugh.

Our house in Soroti was located in a very strategic position, seemingly surrounded by the holy spirits. Early in the mornings, at four o'clock, I would hear a loud noise: "Allah u Akbar." This was the azaan, the Morning Prayer to wake up people in town to gather and pray. Right across from our house was a huge, beautiful Sunni mosque, built with stunning Islamic architecture and surrounded by beautiful gardens that were filled with a variety of fruit trees. Beside the mosque, there was a school, with some boarding facilities as well. Five houses to our right lived Rukyabai, the well-respected elder, and next to her house was the Shia Ithna-asheri mosque. To the left of our house, about four hundred yards away, was a beautiful Hindu temple. Finally, behind our house, around three blocks away, was the beautiful Shia Ismaili mosque, which was the mosque that our family attended.

Across the road from our family's mosque was an upper-class sports club. Outside, the club had two volleyball courts, as well as two beautiful red clay tennis courts surrounded by a fence. The clubhouse included ping-pong tables, badminton courts, and card tables. In the corner of the clubhouse was the Chaganbhai canteen, where we could eat and buy fresh chana bateta and mogo, which is also known as cassava. This sports club was a very important part of my early years, and played an integral role in the development of my tremendous interest in sports.

So, how could a boy from a middle-class family afford to go to an aristocratic club? The answer is very simple; you didn't have to be a member. What would happen was many of the aristocrats would only arrive at the club after 5:30pm, when they had closed their stores. I would go to the club earlier in the day, when there were fewer players at the club, to have a better chance of playing volleyball, in particular. When more players would begin to arrive at the volleyball courts later in the day, I would be gradually pushed back and kicked out of the game. Sometimes, however, a player would have to leave the volleyball game early, and I would gain the chance to fill their spot. The tennis courts at the club, on the contrary, were always hard to penetrate, as only four players could play at one time. To have any chance of playing, I often first had to help out as a ball boy. Fortunately, I had a nephew who would take me to the club during the afternoon on weekends, even when it was scorching hot. My tennis game improved so much because of my nephew; he was a very good tennis player, and he really liked playing with me. But remember, I was the golden boy, always being watched by my sisters and my mother, and they would often refuse to let me go to the club on my own.

During these years, I was not good in school; I would barely pass to move onto the next grade. Next to my house lived the family of Mr. Jusab ladak, who had a daughter, Razia. Razia was in my class at school. She was very pretty, and very smart. Every time Razia got her report card, she would run to show it to my mother. My mother would compliment and congratulate Razia, and give her lots of candies and chocolates.

I remember the last day of school one year, when I decided to turn myself around at school. There was a grand lunch, but it cost five shillings. All of those kids in school who expected a good report card would get their parents to give them five shillings to go to the lunch. I knew that my report card was not going to be very good, but it was not at all difficult for me to get five shillings from my mother. But, at the time, my mother did not yet know about my report card.

It was a delicious lunch. I ate as much as my stomach could handle. Why? Well, I knew that, when I got home, my mother would be angry because of my poor report card, so, in order to save face and respect, I was planning to refrain from eating a few meals at home, thereby publicly displaying the dismay that I had of my poor performance at school.

When I came home after the delicious lunch at school, I went straight to my mother, my face filled with remorse, to give her my report card. My mother did not give me her usual hug. I knew, right away, that Razia had already told my mother that I did not do well on my report card. Tears started flowing from her eyes. Soon, those streaks of huge tears were flowing like a stream trying to meet the river, washing all the make-up from her beautiful face. My mother's hands started shaking, and her face turned; she was clearly agitated. Without hesitation, I hugged her, kissed her, and did not let her go. I told her, "Ma this will be the last time you see a report like this."

A second incident helped to turn around my poor performance at school. One early, sunny Saturday morning, before the store became busy with customers, Mr. Bhutt, the head teacher-disciplinarian at my school, came to see my father. Mr. Bhutt told my dad that the school needed money for upgrades, and wanted to raise funds by organizing a variety show at the only cinema house in town. Mr. Bhutt said to my father that I was a very good public speaker, and that he had wanted to participate in the drama, which he just received a script from India. My dad, knowing that I was not doing well in school, was very reluctant to allow me to participate in the play at the variety show. Fortunately, Mr. Bhutt made a promise to my dad that he would personally look after me at school and, if needed, help to pay for my tuition. With Mr. Bhutt's promise, my dad finally agreed to let me participate at the variety show.

So, there I was, practicing for the play every day! My character in the play was Panaram, the barber. On the day of the show, the cinema house was completely filled, and sold out. The show was very successful. Thirty thousand shillings were raised, and I became an instant star. The next few days following the play were the best; everybody appreciated my performance, and the headmaster held a grand reception for us. Following the play, I became motivated by my performance, as well as Mr. Bhutt's promise to my father, and my academic career blossomed. I became one of the top three students in my class. I also found it easier to gain access to the volleyball courts and tennis courts at the sports club, as more people at the club had come to know and respect me.

One of the things in which, sadly, I was totally unsuccessful, and which haunts me still today, at a time when I am almost dying, is my Arabic. My mother taught all of my sisters to recite the Koran in Arabic, but she did not want me to learn Arabic, since I was the golden boy. My father talked to the mwalimu at the school across from our house about teaching me Arabic. The mwalimu promised my dad that I would soon be able to finally recite the Koran. So, there I was, walking to the classroom at the school across the road, with a nice notebook, pencil and pen, ready to learn Arabic and the Koran. Both of my parents were overjoyed and looking forward to me being able to recite the Koran in Arabic. As the saying goes, if wishes were horses, then beggars would ride.

During my second class, I was sitting in between two boys, both of whom were from wealthy families. They were not keen to learn Arabic and, inevitably, started to create mischief. The mwalimu became distracted, and called the two boys to the front. Since I was sitting in between the two boys, I was also called to the front. The mwalimu whipped the two boys, but made me the recipient of the bulk of the whips, because he knew that my father wanted me to learn Arabic. I immediately went home, crying. My mother became very angry at the mwalimu, and declared, "How can the mwalimu whip my son so much? That's it! He's not going to learn the Koran anymore."

As I live my final days, and as I think of my successes and failures, I believe that the biggest failure in my life was not learning Arabic. My aspirations in life included learning Arabic, and to further study my religion at the Institute of Ismaili Studies (IIS) in London, in order work for an Imam and foster peace, pluralism and unity throughout the Muslim ummah. I am fully confident that if I, the golden boy, had become fluent in Arabic Koranic studies and worked under the guidance of my Imam, I would have made a great difference in the Muslim world.

Today, I see a Muslim world that is divided and filled with internal strife. For Muslims, the present epoch is a period of increasing confusion and delusion, anguish and suffering. This has been characterized by growing assaults that are destroying the physical and intellectual reserves of the Muslim nation. Muslims have the fewest university graduates per capita, the lowest literacy rates for women and men, and the highest unemployment for youths (CNN Faredd Zakaria GPS 2011) Furthermore, a tremendous anti-Muslim campaign has been launched by the Western media, and conservative political and academic lobbies have emerged across the continents of Europe, North America and Asia. The combined Gross Domestic Product of the 22 Arab countries is less than that of Spain. These are all serious challenges which need to be faced by the World, using a positive intellectual and functional approach. Our spiritual leader, Agakhan, has said:

"The West must move away from the idea of wanting to transpose its vision of democracy identically into the Islamic world. This cannot work. The West cannot simply erase 1400 years of Muslim history. Islam is by no

means a contradiction to democracy, quite the contrary.
[6] I see no conflict at all if I go back to the original
construct of the Muslim community and how they dealt
with the issues of leadership."

I have been a religious education teacher for primary,
secondary and post-secondary (alazar) students. Alazar was the
first Muslim University establish in Cairo Egypt. I have always
believed that the glorious Fatimid would come back and Islam
would flourish again, freed from the debilitating effects of
"Islamophobia", but I guess I won't see that happen in my
lifetime; if only I hadn't missed out on a great opportunity to
learn Arabic when I was young.

The bud that was my academic career began to blossom
during my years at secondary school in Soroti. Each secondary
school class had at least 75 to 100 students. Secondary school
was very tough, but I had two very good, intelligent friends;
the three of us would study together. There were three levels of
classes at our school: "A", "B", and "C". Only the top students
in the school were enrolled in the "A"-level classes. The students
who achieved the high grades required to proceed to the
"A"-level classes then needed to maintain exceptional marks in
the "A" classes to gain admission to university. Although I was
often busy studying, I also played cricket, volleyball and field
hockey for the school.

I remember Juma, one of the few black students in our
class, who lived in the boarding facilities at the school adjacent
to the mosque across from my house. "Can I walk with you
home?" Juma often asked me at the end of the school day. "Of
course, yes," I would reply.

One evening, when it was late and growing dark, Juma
asked me to help him out with some mathematics questions,

so I went to his boarding room. What a surprise I had! Juma didn't have any electricity, or any lanterns to give him light to study. For light, all he had was a small lamp, with a wick, that was lit by kerosene. Juma's room was nearly empty, except for a mattress in the corner. Thoughts were running through my mind: "How can he live like this? How can he study like this?" He had very little compared to our family; we had proper electricity, and I had a study table and study lamps.

"What are you having for supper?" I asked Juma, while we studied in his room.

"Nothing today, because my father has not brought any dried cassava or sweet potatoes," Juma answered.

The locals often made thin slices of dried cassava and sweet potatoes by drying them in the sun, and then storing them in a bag. Drying the cassava and sweet potatoes in the sun allowed them to last for a very long time before they spoiled. When the locals ate cassava or sweet potatoes, they would boil them in water, to soften them before eating.

When Juma told me that he didn't have any food to eat, I was really taken aback. I thought to myself, "How is this boy going to live without food and electricity to study? Why is God so cruel to him?" At once, I ran home to my house and told my mother about Juma's boarding room. My parents knew Juma well, and they knew that we were studying together, so my mother gave me a lot of food and a nice lantern to give to Juma. My mother also instructed me to tell Juma that, until his father brought him food from the village, our family would provide him food. Overall, seeing Juma's boarding room taught me a valuable lesson: we should never become too materialistic and look down on people who are in a worse position than us. I nurtured this lesson, and I have always tried my best to help the sick, deprived, desperate, marginalized people around me.

Another interesting thing from my youth worth mentioning is that there was only one barber in Soroti. The barber and my father were best friends; a couple of times a week, after supper, my dad would go to the barber store, which had a small veranda in the front and a cement bench on the side, where all of the secrets of the barber's customers were discussed. Anyway, you would think that it would be easy for me to get the most modern haircut, because of my father's friendship with the barber.

The population of Soroti was mostly Hindus, with only a few Muslims. The Hindi youth were always on top of the fashion and dressing, and long hair was the style at the time. One day, I told my dad that I had to go to the barber for a haircut, and he obliged to my request to have long hair (but he went and the told the barber not to cut it long. When I went to the barber, I told him not to cut my hair short. "Don't worry, I know what cut you want," said the barber. But he went through all of my hair with a razor and almost completely shaved my head!

I got really mad, and asked him, "Why did you cut it so short?"

"Do you know who is paying for your haircut?" the barber replied.

"My dad," I said.

"Well, that's the type of haircut that your dad wants you to have." *Barber replied.*

So, throughout my youth, when it came to dressing and hairstyles, I was, typically, the odd man out amongst my Hindu friends. However, I was rarely laughed at, or ridiculed, because I had excellent grades in school and actively participated in the school's extra-curricular activities. I was always liked by my teachers, as well.

I worked very hard during my final year at secondary school, because I had to study for the "O"-level exams from Cambridge University in England. My hard work was rewarded, as I passed the exams with an "A". My entire family rejoiced, and we celebrated with the slaughtering of a healthy goat; the meat was given to the poor.

"Where should I go to study for the 'A' levels?" This was the question confronting me, as well as my family. My two main options were to either go to Aga Khan Secondary School in Kampala, or to stay closer to home and attend school in Mbala. In the end, my family didn't want the golden boy to live too far away, so it was decided that I would attend Mbale Secondary School.

At school in Mbale, I was living away from home for the first time. It was a new experience, but I enjoyed living on my own away from home. My "A"-level subjects at Mbale Secondary School were physics, chemistry, mathematics, geography, and English. Some of the teachers, it seemed, were not very smart; I don't think the mathematics teacher was actually qualified to teach math. I had a friend who was very smart in mathematics, and he would help the teacher to solve math problems!

Life in Mbale was very different from Soroti. Mbale was a bigger town than Soroti. Mbale had a large population, with a rich, aristocratic, well-educated community. Mbale was also a very social town. It could be very easy to deviate from one's mission in Mbale, and slide into a romantic, carefree life bubbling with alcohol and dance parties. About fifty percent of the students in my class did not graduate with good results in their final year of school, and a lot of them had to repeat their final year, either in the same school, or abroad, namely in England or India. I, on the other hand, graduated from the

"A" levels with very good results. Now, I could prepare for university.

Choosing a university for my academic career was very, very difficult. I was offered a scholarship to go to university in England, to study chemical engineering. However, going abroad to study in England, even on a full scholarship, was out of the question for my family. I was the golden boy, and my family feared that, if I went away to England for school, I would not come back. I was also one of only two Asians who were accepted into the engineering program—chemical engineering was not offered—at the University of East Africa and Nairobi Campus. After much thought and deliberation, I decided to enroll in the Bachelor of Science program at the University of Makerere in Kampala, a choice that was agreeable with my family.

Life at the University of Makerere was quite busy for me. I was creative, though, juggling between several activities, balancing academics, social, sports and fitness in my schedule. Some of my favorite days during university were during the month of Ramadan; one year, I fasted for a record-breaking seventeen days at the university, the longest that I had ever fasted. The girls at the university were what we call the "crème of the crop". A lot of the girls were proud and, initially, quite shy, but it became a lot of fun once they came to know you, especially if you shared common interests. A lot of the students perceived university as their last chance to find a life partner, but, if you looked at it realistically, maintaining a relationship with an intellectual, aristocratic girl was expensive. Every weekend, the girls would make plans to go out, putting a lot of stress on the men, both financially and academically. For me, I was not interested in making any serious commitments to a girl, unless I met someone God sent.

During one summer at Makerere, I was very lucky to be hired for a summer job doing research in the chemistry department at the university, under the guidance of a professor. The job paid well; in fact, before the next semester started, I was able to make a quick trip to London, England. I had a fantastic vacation in the land of our former colonial masters. Wasn't that a smart move?

During my final years at Makerere, the political situation in Uganda deteriorated, culminating in a military coup led by General Idi Amin Dada. This was a dangerous time. One could often hear bombs going off, guns firing, and jets flying overhead in the sky. When Idi Amin Dada led the coup that overthrew the old regime, there was celebration all around the university. Many students rejoiced, and celebrated by climbing army tanks and waving tree branches in the air, or hugging the soldiers. This was a memorable event in my university career. I joined a demonstration with other Makererians at the Parliament Building. To show off our academic might, we put on our academic gowns while we demonstrated. Needless to say, at Makerere in Kampala, I was given a great amount of insight into the political workings of Uganda, and grew especially aware of the deteriorating situation in the country.

I very strongly believe that one should fight until one attains the goal that one has set. In his commencement address to the graduating class of 2005 at Stanford University, Steve Jobs, the late C.E.O. of Apple, said:

"Your work is going to fill a large part of your life, and the only way to be truly satisfied is to do what you believe is great work. And the only way to do great work is to love what you do. If you haven't found it yet, keep looking. Don't settle. As with all matters of the heart, you'll know

when you find it. And, like any great relationship, it just gets better and better as the years roll on. So keep looking until you find it. Don't settle."

After graduation, I received a lot of job offers, as well as an opportunity to pursue my Master's degree in organic chemistry. I ended up accepting a job in the government, as a chemist in an analytical laboratory. I worked on improving the quality of the charcoal that was used in the steel industry, and often helped making charcoal in kilns. I also did research on the charcoal fines, which would be dumped in the garbage after the charcoal had gone bad. The fines have a high nutritional value and could contribute to plant growth; I worked on increasing the productivity of various locally grown vegetables using different amounts of fines. I found this job to be very interesting. Unfortunately, I was not able to see the final results of my work, as I was soon running for my life.

The beautiful Sunni Mosque across the road
from our house in Soroti, Uganda.

Demonstrating (in the hat) for the "common man" in
front of the parliament building during my university
years. My friend, Abdul Hamid, stands to my right.

Receiving my graduation certificate from President
Idi Amin Dada, who was also the Chancellor of
the University of East Africa, Makerere.

Relaxing with my wife, Sultana.

With my Grandson, Ayaan.

With Sultana and our daughter, Alysha.

MATRIMONY AND DIASPORAS

When I was young, I accompanied my parents, along with my uncle and aunt, on a trip to Tanzania to visit my other uncle, who had become sick. I can still remember our trip, traveling around Lake Victoria, taking a ferry to Mwanza, driving to Tabora, and then finally arriving at the village of Ndala, where my uncle lived with his four daughters. When we finally reached their village, I was shocked to see four bicycles outside their house. I wondered, "How come these young, tiny girls know how to ride a bicycle?" Clearly, they were a very well-off family. I was impressed because I did not own a bike, nor did I know even how to ride one. So, when I saw these girls at my uncle's house, I kept a very low profile.

The second oldest girl, Sultana, was very pretty. She taught me how to ride a bike within a day, and she was actually willing to give me her bike to take back home, but there was no room in the car. I immediately liked Sultana, and my mother liked her, too. At the time, however, we were still very young, so nothing beyond friendship would happen between us for a long time.

As a young man at Makerere University, I had great difficulties trying to choose a girl and standing by my decision. My friends certainly didn't help me to decide on one girl; they would always find something negative about the girls I chose, and I could never change their minds. Consequently, I enjoyed seeing a lot of girls without making any serious commitments. It was only during my final year at Makerere that I finally entered into a serious relationship with a girl. But, again, my friends' negativity became a heavy influence: she was four years older than me. Luckily, I think she had gained the sense that I was going to end our relationship, and she struck first, unilaterally untangling the strong bond which we had built up between us. I was a free man once again.

When I graduated from university in 1971, I was almost twenty three years old, and my search for a life partner was becoming quite a stressful journey. However, far more significant problems were arising in Uganda, which had become an increasingly dangerous and unstable country since Idi Amin Dada's takeover of power earlier in 1971, following a military coup. I had actually met Idi Amin Dada on one occasion, during my graduation ceremony in the early 1972 at Makerere University; he was the university's Chancellor and handed out certificates to the graduates at the ceremony. I found it funny that I received my university degree from this humongous, illiterate, completely naïve Chancellor. On a more serious note, I was also struck by Idi Amin Dada's effect on the atmosphere during graduation day. Instead of rejoicing and celebration, my graduation ceremony was a day filled with fear and uncertainty about Uganda.

In spite of the dark mood in Uganda during this turbulent time, I managed to finally find my love. My aunt—my mother's sister—would talk to my mother about one of my uncle's daughters, Sultana, the pretty girl who had taught me how to ride a bicycle years earlier. Finally, one day, my uncle and aunt, accompanied by Sultana, came over to visit my parents. Needless to say, the rest is history: Sultana and I reconnected, fell in love, and got married.

Unfortunately, Idi Amin Dada's regime had profoundly affected everyday life in Uganda; on some days, even leaving my house to go to work was a difficult task. The plight of the Asian population in Uganda was particularly devastating, culminating in Idi Amin Dada's announcement that all Asians living in Uganda must leave the country, which inevitably lead to a mass migration of Asians out of Uganda. In response to the general turmoil in Uganda under Idi Amin Dada's rule, many Asian Ugandans also sought to find refuge all over the world, including Australia, India, England, Malta, the United States and Canada. Many Ugandans had all of their belonging and wealth taken away from them before they left the country, while many others fled with little more than the clothes they were wearing. In sum, Idi Amin Dada's rule had influenced the beginning of an enormous exodus of Ugandans from the country, as well as the subsequent emergence of the Ugandan, Asian Ugandan and Jewish Ugandan Diasporas throughout the world.

Leaving Uganda was a very difficult choice for me and my family. Sultana and I had married only three months earlier, and Sultana was already two months pregnant. I had been working for the Idi Amin Dada government's Ministry of Defense, running the analytical chemistry laboratories in Wandegeya. I had a condominium in Kampala, on top of Kololo hill, which had been provided by the government. However, my parents, my two sisters, my wife and I ultimately decided to flee Uganda, choosing to resettle in Canada.

When our family landed in Montreal, we were treated very well by the Department of Manpower and Immigration. I was so happy and relieved to be safe in Canada, and I will always be grateful to the Canadian government for allowing my parents to live in Canada; otherwise, they might have been trapped in a United Nations camp in Malta, Austria, Holland, or another European country. We were fed, given clothes for the cold Canadian weather, and sent to our new place in Hamilton. Our family was given a two-bedroom apartment, which had already been furnished for us, including a sofa and an old black-and-white television. Although there were six of us, we had sufficient space to live together in the apartment. As we settled into our new lives in Hamilton, November 1972 was coming to an end, and, as expected, the weather was growing cold. Our first winter was upon us, and snow was at our doorstep.

Hamilton Roots

The day following our move to Hamilton, the entire family went to the employment centre to register with a councilor. The councilor assigned to my wife and I gave us a food subsidy of twenty dollars per week. My parents and sisters were given a little bit more from their councilor, because there were four of them. During our meeting, I insisted to be sent to any job interview immediately. With a firm grasp of the reality facing most recent immigrants, our councilor replied: "Don't rush. It may take three to six months to get a job, even for a university graduate like you," However, I persisted, and asked her to find me a job in the chemical industry as soon as possible, even if it was shift work. Recognizing my determination, our councilor was able to book two job interviews for the very next day.

Meanwhile, I had been told that there was going to be a grand rally at the Royal Canuck Hotel that evening, for the upcoming Grey Cup final between the Hamilton Tiger Cats and Saskatchewan Roughriders. I didn't know anything about American football, and the only two things I knew about the game were that the Tiger Cats were playing for the Grey

Cup in their hometown and had reached the Grey Cup for the first time in many years. My wife and I went to the hotel for the rally, joining hundreds of fans who were cheering for the hometown Tiger Cats. To show my support for the home team, I spent two dollars of the food subsidy that we had received that morning on a black and yellow Hamilton Tiger Cats rosette, which I attached to my coat.

The following day, I went to my first interview, which was for a technician position at a grease manufacturing plant. The man who was interviewing me for the job noticed the Tiger Cats rosette on my coat, smiled, and quickly offered his honest opinion of the position. He told me that it was filthy work that wasn't meant for a university graduate. He added that, within a week or two, I would most likely move on to a better job. I responded that I really needed the job, and, in desperation, declared that I would be willing to immediately sign a one-year contract. My interviewer continued to insist that this was dirty work, and refused to offer me the position. He did, however, end our interview on a gracious note: "My friend, you're a qualified and educated person, so you will find a better opportunity elsewhere. Good luck."

I left the grease plant, without a job, and traveled on the Sanatorium bus to my second interview, at Mohawk Hospital Services, which sat atop the hills on the west side of Hamilton. Mohawk Hospital Services had recently opened, providing laundry services for ten hospitals in Hamilton and the surrounding region, and needed someone with a great knowledge of chemicals to develop an effective detergent formula. When I reached Mohawk, I approached the lady at the front desk, who looked at my rosette, smiled at me, and asked, "Who would you like to see?" I replied, "I'm here to see the General Manager, Mr. George Harrison." She directed to me Mr. Harrison's office, where an older man, with blond hair, was waiting. I was about to meet the man who would change my life in this country.

As I look back through my life, and only weeks away from death, I can say with absolute certainty that I have never met a man like Mr. Harrison. Mr. Harrison seemed to be an angel sent by God to look after me and my family. When I walked into his office, I encountered an older man—he looked like he was in his sixties—with blond hair. Mr. Harrison greeted me with a long embrace, and led me to the cafeteria to begin a very strange interview. I handed my resume to Mr. Harrison, but he seemed far more interested in learning about my personal life, asking of the safety of my family and the story of how I left Uganda to settle in Canada. We never discussed the job position.

Following a delicious lunch in the cafeteria, Mr. Harrison gave me a tour of the facilities. As we walked together, Mr. Harrison described, in detail, the complete workings of the new automated system that had been installed. My particular job at Mohawk Hospital Services, he explained, would involve setting up certain formulae for different linens, and setting up special tests on the final rinse of the automated system. Later in the tour, Mr. Harrison told me that he would love to hire me. He understood that I would be able to find employment at many other places of business, and emphasized that I should not feel guilty if I wanted to pursue other job opportunities. To further show his support, Mr. Harrison also offered jobs at Mohawk Hospital Services to any member of my family, church and community.

When we reached the change room, Mr. Harrison stopped walking and asked me if I would, on behalf of my family, accept two bags of warm clothing that were sitting inside the change room. I accepted his kind offer, and went into the change room to find two full bags of almost-new clothing. Mr. Harrison then performed yet another act of exceptional kindness, stating, "I will give you a ride to your apartment, so you don't have to carry these bags on the bus." He added that he wanted the opportunity to meet my family. I was completely taken aback, and waited for a few moments to answer, as I wondered how he would feel when he saw our lousy two-bedroom apartment, with broken furniture, and if he would become uncomfortable around my parents, who did not speak English well. But, thankfully, Mr. Harrison interrupted my thoughts of hesitation with a comforting remark: "I know what you're worrying about; but, don't worry. I started my life just like you." Soon, I was riding in the passenger seat of Mr. Harrison's Lexus. As we rode, I periodically looked over at Mr. Harrison; the more I looked, the more I felt that this man was a Godsend for me in Canada. I could feel the immense human kindness in him. Still, I worried of his possible reaction when he saw my apartment.

After we had reached my building, Mr. Harrison and I climbed the stairs and entered my apartment. I could not believe how Mr. Harrison treated my family. He hugged every member of my family—my parents, two sisters, and Sultana. When my father asked Mr. Harrison his age, I was surprised to hear Mr. Harrison reply that he was fifty-five years old. He remarked that he felt he could work at Mohawk for another ten years. While sitting down on our run-down sofa chair, Mr. Harrison offered to give us furniture, utensils, and a new television. We politely refused; Mr. Harrison had already given us enough to settle into life in Canada. Looking back, I felt like I had entered into a dream world when I walked into Mr. Harrison's office. God had brought a kind, generous man to help me and my family, and to remind me that I was the "golden boy".

That evening, I went to our new mosque, which was a small room in a Salvation Army building, and told the priest to announce to those in attendance that anyone who was interested in working at Mohawk Hospital Services should contact me. Mr. Harrison stayed true to his offer during our meeting; my wife, father, aunt, and my aunt's friend all worked at Mohawk Hospital Services. In fact, my father, my aunt and her friend all worked at Mohawk until they were sixty-five and required, according to Ontario government regulation, to retire.

Following only three weeks on the job at Mohawk, Mr. Harrison called me into his office. Mr. Harrison informed me that an Assistant Professor in chemical engineering at McMaster University, Dr. Benedict, had called him earlier to ask about me. Mr. Harrison then said that Dr. Benedict wanted to offer me a job as a Research Assistant in the chemical engineering department! Mr. Harrison reassured me that I should not worry about leaving my job at Mohawk, and said that I could return to work at Mohawk if I didn't like my new job. He also promised to look after my family and friends who were currently working for him. I could not believe what was happening. With tears in my eyes, I hugged Mr. Harrison, and told him that he was the kindest man I had ever met in my life. Mr. Harrison urged me to keep in touch and call him every week. Truly, Mr. Harrison was unlike any other person I have ever met.

With the help and guidance of Mr. George Harrison, our family's life in Hamilton was safe and secure. In June 1973, my daughter, Saiira, was born. Suddenly, the two-bedroom apartment had become incredibly crowded, and far too small to comfortably accommodate our growing family. As a result, we bought an old two-storey house on Cannon Street, in the Italian section of Hamilton. I had thought if we could live together for a few more years in the apartment on Cannon Street, then we could save a lot of money and gain the opportunity to provide a good life for our children. However, our family depended on one income; Sultana remained at home with our young daughter.

I remained in regular communication with Mr. Harrison following my departure from Mohawk Hospital Services. Mr. Harrison would invite our family for dinner at his house a couple of times every year, and our family would often reciprocate. Mr. Harrison also continued to offer help and guidance. For instance, when I mentioned to him that I was interested in starting an import/export business with Africa in the future, Mr. Harrison offered his own private company to help with business communication, if I ever pursued that venture. On another occasion, Mr. Harrison asked about the rest of my family that had remained in Africa, and if they wanted to move to Canada. I told him that my wife's sister, who lived with her husband and daughter in Dar es Salaam, Tanzania, was thinking of coming to Canada. I added that her husband—my brother-in-law—had a certificate in accounting. Mr. Harrison asked me to tell Sultana's brother-in-law to send his certificate in accounting to Mr. Harrison. After three months passed, Mr. Harrison called me to say that the Immigration Department had phoned him, to find out why he wanted to hire an accountant from Africa, as there were plenty of accountants in southern Ontario. Mr. Harrison then told me that he had replied to the Immigration Department with, to my mind, the most flattering remark: "I would hire every member of this family, because they are the most hardworking people who have ever worked for me. We should have more of these people working in Canada." By the following year,

Sultana's sister and her husband, along with their daughter, had moved to Canada.

When I first met Dr. Benedict at McMaster University, he was quite impressed by my work in chemical engineering in Africa. In particular, Dr. Benedict was interested in my experiments on charcoal and carbon while I was employed with the government of Uganda. I explained to Dr. Benedict that I had discovered a tremendous increase in the yield of beans grown in soil that had been mixed with charcoal fines. Dr. Benedict was clearly impressed with my work, and immediately offered me a job as a Research Assistant. Interestingly, Dr. Benedict's research at the time, similar to my work in Uganda, was focused on charcoal, namely experimenting with activated charcoal in water treatment. Dr. Benedict then asked me how many days it took for me to find my first job in Canada; I replied that it took only three days. Dr. Benedict could not hide his admiration of my accomplishments in Canada during such a short period of time.

Working as a Research Assistant was a valuable experience. Although the pay was not exceptional, I enjoyed a wealth of opportunities at the university: I could enroll in courses for free, attend conferences, publish my research, and use the gymnasium, squash, tennis courts and swimming pool. I also had the chance to work with graduate and postdoctoral students on many occasions. This was an ideal job for me in a number of ways. However, Research Assistants depended on grants to remain employed; if the research grants ever dried up, I would have been out of luck. Fortunately, I never had to experience any severe hardships in finding and maintaining employment. Following four years as a Research Assistant at McMaster University, I left for a job at Canada Center for Inland Waters in Burlington, where I worked for two years, until I received an offer to become the Supervising Chemist at Stelco. I would spend the rest of my working career at Stelco.

Life in Hamilton offered its share of ups-and-downs, though I never became too distracted to stop going to the gym, playing tennis, or taking part in other sports to relieve stress and tension. My family, especially my mother, insisted that Sultana and I have another baby; perhaps, a "golden boy". In June 1979, after a few years had passed following Saiira's birth, our second daughter, Alysha, was born. In spite of some financial hardship, our family did everything we could to provide our children with the best possible life, and to never deprive them of any educational, recreational, or religious opportunities. To save money, we would take our vacations with a limited budget; once, when we went on a vacation down-south, we traveled by car.

Thankfully, with the additional support of my parents, our two daughters blossomed into well-educated and well-mannered teenagers. Saiira and Alysha were both very involved in public speaking, debating, religious recitals and sports. Saiira enjoyed being on her own, and living independently. She completed her Bachelor of Arts at the University of Windsor, and aspired to become a lawyer. Unfortunately, Saiira had always found mathematics difficult, which became a hindrance when she took the LSAT exam, a required test for applicants to law school. Saiira's low scores on the math portion of the LSAT exam affected her overall score on the exam, and prevented her from acceptance to law school. However, she continued to fight for admission, in spite of her LSAT scores. Alysha was quite different from Saiira. Alysha was very sharp in mathematics, a people-person, and had a lot of friends. After graduating from Ryerson University, Alysha soon embarked on a career in banking in Mississauga.

As Saiira and Alysha grew into young women, we moved out of our two-bedroom apartment and into our first house, on the older side of the main road that was located in the hills of Hamilton. Soon after, we moved into a new residential area in the hills. When my two sisters had both married, I moved my parents into a small bungalow. Finally, Sultana and I sold our house in Hamilton, and bought a house in Mississauga, near Kennedy Road. For the first time during our time in Canada, we had moved away from Hamilton.

Diagnosis and the Beginning of the ALS Tsunami

On Saturday, August 17, 2008, our family's attention was centered on Alysha's pregnancy. Alysha was due to give birth at any moment, and she had been experiencing stomach pains that morning. I had gone to work at the Laundromat that morning, though I was very anxious about Alysha's condition. Then, finally, as I was driving back home from the Laundromat that afternoon, I received a phone call from my wife, who joyfully told me that Alysha had just given birth to a baby boy! I was so ecstatic that I nearly jumped out of the driver's seat of my car. I could barely control my excitement during my drive to Credit View Hospital, to greet my newborn grandson, Ayaan.

On that glorious day, God provided so many miracles. God had granted my late mother's wish for Alysha to have a son. Alysha and her grandmother had been extremely close; Alysha had always been devoted to helping me take care of my mother until she passed away. God had also satisfied the desire of Alysha's husband, Imran, and his family to add another member to their family. For me, God had consented to my wish for a grandson. I couldn't believe how lucky I was that day. As I drove down the highway, the usual heavy traffic on the highway had miraculously disappeared. The weather, which had been unrelentingly dreary, cloudy and rainy for the entire day, all of a sudden gave way to a bright, sunny afternoon. After reaching the hospital in Mississauga, I was soon holding my seven-pound grandson. Ayaan's eyes were wide open, staring around the room, as if he already knew everyone around him. At that moment, I was convinced that this boy was very special.

Soon after Ayaan's birth, Sultana and I decided to move to Woodbridge, into a semi-detached house. Our place was now much closer to Alysha's family; they had already moved into a house in Woodbridge, after Alysha had been promoted to work at the bank's headquarters in Markham. We found Woodbridge to be a clean, relatively unpolluted city, and an ideal place to raise a family. When the weather was nice, I would take Ayaan to the park in a baby-buggy. Ayaan was a delightful baby to be around; whenever we were together, I enjoyed his sweet smiles and infectious giggles.

Around the time of our move to Woodbridge, however, I was beginning to realize that I felt physically weakened performing everyday tasks. When my friend, Nabi, and I played tennis, I found it gradually became harder for me to keep up with him. I was growing tired sooner in our games, and my skills seemed to be regressing. One day, I noticed I could not effectively use my hands to button my shirt. On another occasion, when Sultana and I were packing our belongings in Mississauga for our move to Woodbridge, I had a difficult time carrying boxes from the basement to the garage. In fact, I experienced pains in my back, as well as in my spinal cord, for the first time that day. I remember thinking, with frustration, "Since when did lifting heavy weights hurt my back?" I told my neighbour in Mississauga about the troubles I was having with my hands and back. My neighbour, who had undergone carpal tunnel surgery on his left hand, believed that I had probably developed a similar ailment in my hands. Concerning my back, he said that I probably developed an injury from over-exercising at the gym. He recommended that I visit a doctor in Woodbridge. With worrying thoughts racing through my mind, I agreed, and sought to find a doctor.

I was able to find a walk-in clinic that was close to our new house in Woodbridge. At the clinic, the General Practitioner gave me some painkillers, and suggested that I take B-12 injections to alleviate the pains in my back. Also, to make sure that my hand aches and back pains were not serious, the General Practitioner advised me to book an appointment to undergo an MRI at a hospital. He also booked a separate appointment for me to see a neurologist. Unfortunately, my appointment with the neurologist wouldn't be for another two months. In the meantime, I continued with my regular exercises at the gym, working through body aches that seemed to only become worse. By the time of my appointment, walking long distances had become a great challenge, the weakness in my right leg had doubled, and my general stability had worsened.

When Sultana and I finally went to see the neurologist, he quickly concluded that I had carpal tunnel syndrome and, to correct the pain, arranged to send me to the plastic surgeon to undergo a simple procedure on my left hand. In hindsight, it is quite clear that the neurologist's initial diagnosis was wrong; I never recovered from the surgery on my hand. However, going into the surgery, which took only a few minutes, I assumed that I would soon have my right hand corrected as well, once I had recovered from the first surgery on my left hand. At the time, I guess nobody understood the severity of my health condition.

The neurologist also informed me that I had to book a separate appointment to examine the escalating pains in my right leg. Following his instruction, I immediately returned to the General Practitioner at the clinic and booked a second appointment with the neurologist. It would take another two months before I could see the neurologist again! Meanwhile, I could not comprehend what was happening to my right leg. As the days passed leading up to my second appointment, the pains in my right leg worsened. When I went for my second visit to the neurologist, I could feel substantial muscle weakness; every time I moved my toes, it felt like I had snorkelling fins on my feet. The neurologist used an electromyogram—EMG, for short—which can detect abnormal muscle activity in a number of diseases and conditions, including muscular dystrophy, inflammation of muscles, pinched nerves, peripheral nerve damage (damage to nerves in the arms and legs), myasthenia gravis, disc herniation and amyotrophic lateral sclerosis, also known as Lou Gehrig's disease. Then, he instructed me to do sit-ups and push-ups with electrons connected to my body. When the neurologist asked if I had been experiencing a twitch, I did not understand his question; I didn't even know what he meant by twitching. After the tests, the neurologist still could not give a diagnosis, and he told me to book another appointment for further examination. The earliest appointment was in three months.

When Sultana and I visited the neurologist for a third time, I went through the same tests again. At last, he gave me his diagnosis: "I'm not entirely sure, but it seems that you are showing symptoms of pseudo-ALS, also known as Lou Gehrig's disease." I knew Lou Gehrig was a baseball player, but I had never heard of ALS or Lou Gehrig's disease. As soon as my appointment had finished, Sultana and I rushed home to search the internet for information on ALS. We were shocked to find out that ALS was a devastating and fatal disease. My family urged me to go to the General Practitioner, to get a second opinion on my condition. At the walk-in clinic the next day, the General Practitioner was surprised to hear the neurologist's diagnosis. He told me to contact the ALS Society of Ontario.

When I called the ALS Society, they were very kind and welcoming, and immediately booked an appointment for me to meet the head of the ALS Society, Dr. Zimmerman, at the ALS clinic, at Sunnybrook Hospital. After undergoing an EMG and some other tests, Dr. Zimmerman confirmed that I had ALS. He showed me the results of my breathing test, which indicated that my lung capacity was already down to 60 percent. Dr. Zimmerman then told me that the sleeping test showed that I definitely had a breathing problem, so, in order to have a decent sleep, I needed to be hooked onto a bi-pape at night. He concluded our conversation by informing me that I could not participate in any new medication trials, because my disease was too far advanced. I couldn't help thinking about the two years of my life that were wasted while I waited on the neurologist to diagnose my condition.

As I drove home from my appointment with Dr. Zimmerman, my thoughts kept going back to one particular question: "Is this really true?" I could not comprehend what was happening, or how my muscles could be gradually decimating into rubble. I had treated my body well for a long time; I never had a heavy meal after six o'clock in the evening. I exercised regularly. I went to the gym two to three times a week, played competitive tennis once a week, and ran three to five miles once a week. My physical fitness was the envy of many people at the mosque. When my friends learned of my battle with ALS, they were shocked and frightened; if this could happen to a well-disciplined and physically fit person, then this could happen to anyone.

One morning, I looked into the bathroom mirror before going into the shower, and noticed the muscles around my chest and forearms were twitching. My motor neurons had died, causing my poor muscles to lose control. I had built and maintained my muscles for years, through a combination of weightlifting, playing tennis and squash, running on the treadmill, doing leg presses, and other forms of exercise. Now, my body was rapidly breaking down, weakening as each day passed. I wasn't too far away from becoming a palliative care patient and, ultimately, disappearing from this world.

My first visit to the ALS clinic at Sunnybrook at the beginning of 2010 had been useful and eye-opening, but subsequent visits became too long and accomplished very little. The disease was progressing rapidly. To accommodate the worsening state of my condition, the ALS society provided most of the equipment and furniture that I was beginning to require in everyday life.

During the summer of 2010, I could still handle common physical tasks; I didn't require assistance showering, going to the toilet, or getting dressed. I was able to get around using a walker. With the aid of a walker, I was still able to go out with my family, go shopping, attend to our business at the Laundromat, and carry out exercises at the gym. Climbing the stairs had become increasingly difficult, so we had a stair-case lift installed in our house. All I had to do on the lift was press a button to take me up or down the stairs.

In September, I noticed that I needed to either keep the air-conditioner running constantly, or crack the window open, in order to breathe without difficulty. As the weather turned colder, I found that breathing had become even more challenging. Then, one day in October, my health suddenly took a significant turn for the worse. I was rushed to Humber Finch Hospital, where I was diagnosed with acute pneumonia.

The pneumonia, along with two bouts of diarrhea, destroyed my muscle strength and stamina. I was losing the desire to live any longer. My life was being washed away by the ALS tsunami.

In early 2011, after spending two and a half months in the Intensive Care Unit, I was finally sent home. I was assigned a Personal Support Worker, as I could not walk, stand, or use my hands to eat. My family was told that I was expected to live for only two more weeks. But, here I am, one year later, still alive and fighting. I couldn't have done it without the constant support of my wife, daughter, and the PSW.

Due to my acute breathing problem, I am dependent on bi-pipe support twenty-four hours a day. As a result, I am not able to leave my house. I have not seen the sun, the moon, the stars, or my neighborhood for over a year. Indeed, relying on support for breathing requires a total change of boundaries. Using the bi-pipe was also far less comfortable than it should have been. When I had first gone to the ALS clinic to learn how to use the bi-pipe, I was not informed of the benefit of using nose plugs, which would have assisted my breathing while I was talking or eating. I was given only a compact mask that covered my mouth and prevented me from talking and eating comfortably. Whenever it was time to eat, I had to remove the mask and eat my food very quickly, because I had troubles breathing if I wasn't wearing the mask. I was unable to simply enjoy my meals. We all know that ALS sufferers are going to die, so, why not let them live a comfortable life during the time they have left?

An important reason for my desire to write my memoirs is to publicize how little people know of ALS. During the last four years, since I first learned that I had ALS, I have seen an advertisement about ALS on TV only once. This is extremely unfortunate, considering that about three thousand Canadians are currently suffering from this disease. I believe that Canadians need to be better informed of this deadly disease. A greater emphasis on raising public awareness of ALS would almost certainly lead to more opportunities for fundraising. Furthermore, doctors need to have a much better understanding of ALS. When I told my physician friends that I had ALS, many of them admitted that they had little knowledge of this neurological disease. Looking back, it took two years for my neurologist, whom the General Practitioner at the walk-in clinic recommended, to correctly diagnose my condition. I think it's critical for neurologists to be better educated in ALS, and to develop an updated tool for properly diagnosing this disease. There is so much more that can be done to battle ALS.

WHO AM I?

The other day I read quote from Steve Jobs

> *"Your time is limited, so don't waste it living someone else's life.*
>
> *Don't be trapped by dogma—which is living with the results of other people's thinking.*
>
> *And most important, have the courage to follow your heart and intuition.*
>
> *They somehow already know what you truly want to become.*
>
> *Everything else is secondary . . . ."*

As I lay on my bed waiting for my last breath and with the ventilator pushing air to the diaphragm into my lungs and keeping me alive, I'm thinking to myself who am I, and what have I done? As the singer Jim Reeves says "*This world is not my home I'm just passing through*". Have I touched anybody? Have I lifted a fallen comrade? Have I made a failing kid to excel academically?. In summary have I helped this world?. The above quote from the address to the graduating class at Stanford University by Steve Jobs very well summarizes my thoughts.

I have always believed that an empty mind is the devil's workshop. All evil actions starts in the vacant mind. Keep your mind occupied in something positive, something worthwhile. Actively follow a hobby. Doing something that holds your interest. You must decide what you value more: money or peace of mind. Your hobby, like social work or religious work, may not always earn you more money, but you will have a sense of **fulfillment and achievement**. Even when you are resting physically, occupy yourself in healthy reading or mental chanting of God's name.

Very often I have noticed the solution to many of my problems suddenly appears in my mind in the middle of my prayers in the jamatkhana (mosque) in the midst of the service. So often I would be calling somebody in the middle of the night to discuss the solution. This might seem strange to some, but this was the gift from God to me.

Very confidently I can say that I have a vision. I have a very thinking analytical inquisitive brain which leads to unabated pursuit of my goals. Some people say to me because of this, I have lost my motor neurons and have succumbed to this neurological disorder.

B) Hamilton

When I'm dead and people come to know that Anver najak died. People will say which Anver najak "Hamilton, Varo" meaning the guy from Hamilton. This is how lots of people from Canada know me as the guy from Hamilton who organized traditional volleyball and basketball tournament. I used to organize volleyball tournaments and invite teens across Ontario to Hamilton. This is the massive undertaking for a community of only about 200 people leaving in Hamilton and providing food accommodation and etc. to 140 participants was not an easy task.

I arranged for regular local gym facilities for the entire congregation for swimming, volleyball, table tennis, badminton, yoga, and physical fitness programs.

In fact participants from Niagara Falls, Branford, Halton and Hamilton used to join us for much needed physical fitness programs. I was a member for youth for a very long time for Hamilton and I made sure that the team which we assembled for annual sports festival was a well respected and strong team, thereby making Hamilton known as fitness capital for Ismail community in Ontario.

I had establish a very good contact with the trophy dealer in Hamilton and used to purchase trophies and award for all sporting events for Toronto for a very cheap price. Unfortunately or fortunately one day when I went to pick up the order, the owner told me that he was filling for bankruptcy very soon and I would lose the deposits unless I came to pick up for whatever is left in the store at night. I went to his store and picked up a small manual engraving machine, some trophy parts and took them to my basement and started making trophies without any training or professional help. The business blossomed. Soon I had no time to provide trophies for other communities. I bought computerized engraving machine and upgraded the quality of the awards. The work I did was for my community in Canada. I used to supply trophies all the way from Montreal in the east to Alberta in the west. I used to make creative design, creative medals and especially for our community. Thus the community had to pay only cost price for the awards. My awards came very popular across Canada and soon the religious education department and other portfolio's started ordering from me. I'm still wondering who gave me this idea and who gave me this creativity.

During my stay in Hamilton I used to play tennis in indoor bubble and I always thought how I can bring youths and interested adults to come and join the club. They found it very expensive to join and I came up with very inexpensive idea, whereby on regular basis I would rent the bubble and invite these people to come and play tennis at subsidized cost. I would arrange free coaching session from professional coaches working at the club and celebrate the evening with pizza and pop. This was very successful even today I see a lot of youths I used to train play tennis on regular basis.

As you drive along the stone church road on the east mountain, camouflage behind the banquet center, surrounded by beautiful evergreen trees is the Hamilton Jamatkhana (mosque) which was almost not built. Previously Hamilton Jamatkhana was located Downtown on Barton street in a high risk neighborhood. The city was prepared to give us the land on the mountain if we started building Jamatkhana within a year at a subsidize rate. Nobody for a long time was interested in moving Jamatkhana to the mountain except for a few people. A warning was issued by the city that if you don't buy the land soon, we will lose the deal. Eight of us put in 100,000 dollars together to start building the Jamatkhana.

"You can always be successful when there is a desire to serve others."

unknown

As the above quote tells us very explicitly that true desire always reaps fruits in the same way we started the construction of a new jamatkhana. Later on we met some rich and very kind members of Toronto congregation who lend us money without interest for five years. Today the Jamatkhana is fully paid and it is an icon of jamatkhanas worldwide and I'm very proud to be a part of this project.

I was a chairman of religious education portfolio for Hamilton for a while and used to teach religious education to the secondary school students, made sure that all the religious ceremonies were held according to the protocol. As I enter the final phase of my journey, I see a lot of the students whom I taught have excelled academically and spiritually. I believe in order for kids to absorb religious knowledge, the training has to start at very young age, at which time entertainment aspect as also got to be added. Thus I used to organized religious hymes recitals (ginans) and public speaking competitions (waezes).

My daughters were getting tired of just basic religious education and therefore I used to take them to Toronto to attend special programs so as to interact with more teenagers from our Toronto mosques such as Juniour waezeen program. I used to attend Etobicoke Jamatkhana whenever I got a chance with my children. One day while driving to Etobicoke my daughter Alysha said "Dad one day, why don't we go to Halton Jamatkhana, my friend always tell that we should go so that we can see the Jamatkhana". One Friday we went to Halton Jamatkhana, hidden behind the Bronte provincial park in the midst of commercial buildings was the small picturesque Halton Jamatkhana. We used to visit that Jamatkhana quite often. During one of the visit I met a woman whom I called AZ, a very intelligent, honest, devoted and creative thinking person. While talking to her I found her to have similar vision as mine as far as imparting knowledge both religious and secular to the members of our congregation. This was like I hit a jackpot. Finally I met somebody who would help to propagate and share the vision I have for my community in general and youths in particular. While I am narrating my good old times, it would seem I am a normal person. But I just remembered that I only have very a short time left to live. My thighs had been totally destroyed and just looked like bone, which usually is given to a dog. My hands are completely dead. My breathing is becoming harder and harder even with the help of the ventilator. I don't know when it will stop completely and my soul would be separated from my body.

Etobicoke Jamatkhana (mosque) became my usual Friday jamatkhana and I was told to start teaching Microsoft office by the leadership in a small computer room which had five computers but only three of them were working. When I went to check out a computer class, I found something very strange. The computers were not used for a long time, and I could see from the small window in the door. A long line up of youths staring at me trying to find out what was going on. I also noticed large clusters of youths hiding near the shoe rack area in corners outside in the hall, when prayers are going on inside the mosque, I very vividly remember after finishing higher school certificate (A level) in Mbale in Uganda I had four months vacation before the start of the University. Instead of staying home and doing nothing I got a job as a high school teacher in a private school in my hometown. On my last day before leaving for the University the headmaster (principal of the school) called me in his office and said "Mr. Najak you are a bright young men and don't forget the three D's, **Discipline, Dignity, and Decency**. This will lead you to the straight path to success". I remembered the headmasters words and knew right away that the kids are missing one of the **D's.** I came to the conclusion that nobody was looking after these activities for the youths, nobody to guide them so I embarked on projects to stimulates the youths academically and socially. I myself have been a good public speaker and often used to attend the downtown Toronto Toast Masters Club. I brought this issue about Etobicoke youths and was advised to carry out TOAST MASTERS PUBLIC SPEAKING FOR THE YOUTHS PROGRAM. It was a three months course whereby participants meet once a week. The Toast Masters Club offered me full co-operation by giving me qualified trainer and training material at no cost. I brought this issue up with priest in the mosque and they completely agreed with me and found me a donor who would subsidize the rental of conference room in a four star hotel near the mosque for the duration of the cost. AZ recruited the participants for the course. Right on the first day sitting in a conference room, with the jug of water and glasses, spaced on the tables, notepads, and pen for each participant, totally amazed participants. The participants were very excited and they have never witness a welcome like that before. Adrenalin started flowing in the veins of the participants and the level of participation was unbelievable. This program was very successful. Meanwhile I was appointed the manager for special projects for education board for Ontario under the chairmanship of Fiaz Basaria. Other Mosque in the east end requested me to organize similar program at their Mosque. We organize similar programs to mosques in the east end and promoted the program by using the following script.

"Rozmin had applied for a position as one of the director for this International Company and this was her final interview. She was to be interviewed by a group of directors and CEO's for this position. Rozmin had put on a beautiful dress she bought from the boutique and looked very beautiful with the expensive make up for this interview. Everybody was seated in the conference room and Rozmin was asked "why should we give this job to you and not somebody else?" Rozmin was a very smart person but as she stood to answer the question her fingers started to tremble, and her ears started to change color. Small droplets of sweat started to build up on her beautiful face, she started to shake. As time went on the droplets grew bigger and bigger and rolled out on her cheeks like small streams carrying with it the expensive make-up she had put on, just like the Nile river carrying the silt and depositing on the delta. Soon her neck was filled with make-up and sweat and she thought in her mind **"I wish i had attended Toast Master Course at Etobicoke".**

By this time the congregation in Etobicoke knew that I was a very creative person who had dedicated his time for the upliftment of the youths of Etobicoke. My friends were very thrilled by my programs and told me the story about the cow and the pig. This is how it goes, let me tell you a little story of a rich Goan landlord who once asked his parish priest. Why does everybody call me stingy when everyone knows that when I die I will leave everything I have to this church.

The priest said, there once was a pig and a cow in this village. The pig was unpopular and the cow was loved by all in the village. This puzzled the pig. The pig said to the cow, people speak warmly of your good nature and your helpful attitude. They think you are very generous because each day you give them milk, butter and cheese. But what about me? I give them everything I have. I give them the famous

Goa sausages, bacon and ham. I also provide ingredients for mouth-watering sorpotel. Yet no one likes me. Why is that? The priest continued do you know what the cow answered? The Cow said, perhaps it's because I give, while I am still living.

My motor neuron were all alive and controlling my muscles really well, I was physically very fit and I thought this was the time to help the youths. The rejuvenation of the youths desire to uplift themselves was now very visible. I had tremendous parental support. My daughter Alysha was also at the age whereby she could assist in developing creative programs.

The leaders of the Jamatkhana told me that there was great deficiency in the congregation in computer skills and that I should start classes to teach the young and old Microsoft office. So with four working computers and the youths bubbling with the desire to learn Microsoft power point, I started the classes for the youths. I got donations for two televisions' which were hooked in the hallways. I bought VGA to TV convertor and connected to the television and taught the kids how to have a power point slide show running continuously on the television. The youths were totally amazed and volunteered to run every Friday's announcements for the mosque on the television. The entire congregation was very thrilled to see such a great advancement of technology of Etobicoke coming from the youths who previously were dormant, as time went by more and more registered for this course. Adults wanted to upgrade their skills in excel word and PowerPoint, the only hindrance being the lack of computer. Following is the letter written by one of the students whom I mentored and is currently doing his PHD at Harvard University.

Hello Najak Uncle,

I'm so sorry to hear about your illness. As you know, our whole family supports you in our thoughts and prayers.

If there is any consolation to illness, though, it's that you can see so plainly how many people around you care deeply for you. However close your family and friends are to you now is surely a testament to how close you've been to them all along, to how much you've provided and cared for them.

Personally, I know that I would never be as academically successful, as self-confident, as critical a thinker, as social a person were it not for the guiding hand you had in my adolescence. The care and love you showed me and my generation at Khane provided us with not just skills (I remember clearly when I first learned power-point to use on the two TVs at the back of khane! And when I first improvised a speech on 'flowers' our first day at Toastmasters!) but also with a sense of community, a sense of purpose, a sense of confidence. Your selfless mentorship pushed all of us to make something of ourselves. You really believed in us and that helped me believe in myself. I remember every Junior Achievement class, every time I practiced my speech for the speech competition in Edmonton. In those many tiny ways, you helped me become who I wanted to be in the world. I owe you so much, truly. You should take comfort in knowing that so many of us will continue to mentor other students, to do for them what you did for us.

Just wanted to say – as if you don't know already – that we're all thinking of you and hoping for the best. I hope to come and see you in February after I return home from Paris. Khushiali Mubarak.

Latif

<u>Parliamentary style debating, Spelling Bee, junior achievement business program.</u>

I found that the youths were not involved in the country's political system. So as to expose them to the political system and show them what is going on in the Parliament I embark on a project and enrolled the youths and seniors in a parliamentary style debating forum, we had the government headed by the prime minister and two of his ministers. (The ministers are chosen depending on motion brought about by the opposition) The opposition was led by the leader of opposition and two of his shadow members (depending on motion brought about by the opposition) when I contacted the toast masters about this project they were totally thrilled and I could sense the exuberance and excitement to their veins. They brought in well trained toast masters from the downtown toast master club and conducted this one month course. The final debate took place in the hall outside the Jamatkhana Etobicoke, so the entire congregation could attend and enjoy this event. The pompous entry into the house of political parties and the speaker of the house followed by volunteers of the mosque dressed up as security guards resembling RCMP was carried out. The entire congregation loved this very much and gave a standing ovation when the entry into the parliament was made. The success of this program spread like wild fire to other Jamatkhana in the GTA and they wanted us to repeat event in their Jamatkhana but it was too much for the Toast Master to repeat this course so instead we took the debate to few of the Jamatkhanas. Pickering Jamatkhana was so thrilled they formed their own team involving the seniors and the youths and ask for my assistance to train them. I had never met a enthusiastic group like that and the debate in the Jamatkhana was very successful. These were the good old days when I was bubbling with energy, exuberance, to lift the member of my congregation and made sure they excel in their academic years.

Spelling bee is often referred to as a program to enhance the spelling capability of a student. A stimulating educational program, outside the regular school curriculum, which would focus specifically on English language basics. Under the auspices of education board special projects team. This project was launched in Etobicoke, Jamatkhana with a lot of assistance from AZ and her team in fact it would be wrong to say that under the leadership of AZ this program was a real success. The booklets containing the list of words to be spelled, rules and regulation and other important information where all prepared by her teammate and were given out to the registered participants.

The concept of spelling bee started in United States of America and then spread to various countries in the Americas including Canada. Every year a grand spelling bee competition is held in United States, televised on ESPN and dominated by Southeast Asian youths. It seems this very important concept of spelling bee has been completely ignored the recent years and Etobicoke together with Scarborough youths were the only ones who benefited from this. Well I think it's time for the leadership to revisit this important concept after looking at advancement of Southeast Asian in the United States, good luck.

As I had planned to retire with the small business to keep me busy, I thought to myself "what if plan A fails, I should have a back-up'. There was a part time returning officer for peel region election Canada job offer. I thought I should apply for it, since I have been always involved in election Canada. I applied together with hundreds of other people and after two interviews, only four of us were selected for the final interview.

The final interview was divided into two parts. In the morning we were interviewed by a panel of leaders of election Canada and I did very well in the interview. The afternoon session consisted of writing short paragraphs on the computer.

I am a fast typist, but the only drawback is that I leave behind a lot of spelling mistakes but Bill Gates is very nice to me and he has installed spell check to help people like me.

In the afternoon I started answering the questions and I found no red underline in any of my answers. I finished answering all the questions and only had couple of minutes to review. "WHAT A BOMBSHELL" to my surprise I found spelling mistakes but no red underlines and I pressed the spell check button, IT WAS TOTALLY GREYED OUT. Election Canada was testing my spelling capabilities, to no surprise I did not get the job. Well I didn't care but it would have been another feather on my hat, so now you know how important spelling bee is.

Junior Achievement Corporate Business Plan

Junior Achievement is the world's largest organization dedicated to inspiring and preparing young people to succeed in glow show students how the best way to really learn is to really do. A business of our own engages elementary school students in activities to apply their knowledge and skills to a real life situation.

Junior Achievement is an exciting opportunity for students to demonstrate the teamwork, leadership, and innovative thinking that will help them drive success in the business world.

The member for economic in the council approach me via the education board to explore the possibilities of running a toastmaster junior achievement corporate business program since the youths of Etobicoke have been very successfully motivated by previous programs by me. After a long discussions I accepted this challenge. Once again the donor to help us to rent the conference room at the hotel was ready. We embarked on a recruitment drive, electing the president, secretary, treasurer, accountant, buyer, advertising and promotion person, helpers and members without portfolio from the participants. I thought this was the best way to let the youths run the company themselves, youths as far away as Markham, Brampton, and Mississauga registered for this program and there was a waiting list for participants to join in.

This was a challenging task as we were constantly monitored by the supervisor from toastmaster and the only way I thought to win the award would be to run the company very efficiently and declare very good dividends at the end. Therefore the sales have to be very high and also the profit margin. The company was called BIG UP BASKET and the basket was stuffed with Christmas goodies. All this was done by the participants, led by the president of the company, an excellent opportunity to double up entrepreneurship. Learning accounting by itself is pretty boring so I thought the best way to motivate the business team was to bring a real life very successful chartered accountant from our community. This was a total hit, I had my friend Hanif from Bayview Jamatkhana (the hub of entrepreneur) invite chartered accountants who provided an excellent presentation and as the business owners if they ever needed any help just to contact him. The interest in the company had sky rocketed. The sales exploded and the explosion gave rise to tons of smiles of the participants and injected more enthusiasm. Thus I invited more talented speakers from the community and one of them was the ex-president of the council and very successful entrepreneur who gave his own experiences and thoughts to youths never to give up and how to succeed in business, Mr Aziz Bhaloo (currently serving as AKDN business representative in Nairobi Kenya). Advertising and promotion personnel made eight feet by four feet banner of big up basket in attractive red color. It was very conspicuous and attracted lots of customers, the malls, streets and etc. On the final day at the CBC auditorium downtown Toronto in front of hundreds of participants and other companies, junior achievement board members, our company was declared the most successful company of the year. University scholarships were given to the president of our company, this brought about a very successful and one the most creative programs I had organize when my motor neuron were still connected to my muscles.

At Etobicoke I carried out other creative programs such as quizzes for children, debates and helped out in the BUI (Bait ul Ilm), open house parents night, this was not worth mentioning in detail since God had created me just to help out the world.

<u>Trip to Alberta for participating in the public speaking forum in October 1998 "Leading the Jamat to the Millennium"</u>

If I have to choose the highlight of my analytical brain, creativity, leadership skill, technique for imparting knowledge, intuitive and demonstrating public speaking skills. This program was the one. The Alberta council invited all of Canada for this very innovative speech for the early and late secondary, post secondary, alumni members of the Canadian Jamat. As usual I was contacted by the youth and education board to come up with the strategy on how to select the top students without any bias or favoritism from our community's population of around 50,000. The area to be covered was from Ottawa to Windsor Ontario. I set a committee with the help of AZ and we drafted a very good presentation to the joint youth, education board. We divided into

A. East Ontario—Belleville, Ottawa, etc.
B. Scarborough—Pickering, Oshawa, and Ajax.
C. Don Mills—headquarters, Greenland and thorncliffe
D. Unionville, Bayview, and York Mills.
E. Etobicoke—Mississauga, Brampton and Dundas West.

Since this was a national competition, I felt the participants should be acclimatized to the public speaking format before selecting the top three participant for each region. To accommodate this training to participants dispersed in such a large region, it would be impossible to send a trained toastmaster to each region. Therefore I decided to hold one class with a very well trained toastmaster and video recorded the training and sent a copy of the recording to each coordinator for each region. Thus all the participants get a equal opportunity to understand the subject and prepare accordingly. Together with the toastmaster, we made a judging criteria and sent the criteria to the coordinators and also to the organizer in Alberta (the coordinators in Alberta were not even prepared, and were very thankful to receive the criteria from us.) All the regional competitions were held on the same day and at the same time at all the regional centers, hence nobody would be able to copy any material from any speaker, and this was a win win situation. After selecting the top students, I had to worry about the transportation that some of the students could not afford to fly, the council stepped in and helped out those needy but intelligent ones.

Here is a letter of Thanks from the winner of upper secondary division Farah Nasser. Currently she is a reporter, news reader for City Pulse T.V in Toronto.

Dear Najak Uncle

I am sorry to hear you are sick. In our religion we say, what you do in this life will help you in the next life. If this is the case, I have no doubt there is a special place for you in heaven. You have touched so many people including myself.

Just say two words - "Najak Uncle" in Etobicoke Jamat Khana and every young person has a story to tell about how you have impacted their lives, in fact your are everyone's Najak Uncle.

For me I will never forget the speech competition in Edmonton, Alberta. Your persistence, leadership, hard work and vision allowed many of us to meet our brothers and sisters from across the country for the first time and compete in the public speaking realm. This experience gave us confidence and made me realize how much I enjoy public speaking and this is something I now do professionally.

Thanks to you an entire generation was given opportunities they normally wouldn't have in the most important years of their development. The next generation needs a Najak Uncle, but there is no one else like you. We pray for your good health, joy, happiness in this world and the next!

Thank you Najak Uncle for being you!
Farah Nasser

A team from Ontario did very well so that the congregation in Ontario is not deprived of the speeches, arrangement were made with the religious and education board to allow these winners to give their speeches at all major Jamatkhanas in Ontario. The congregation was really touched by this gesture and the council, parents and students really thank me for this. Lots of these children have now become leaders, excelled in their careers and some are still continuing their education, thus this experience was an experience of a lifetime.

Year 2004 to Present

I always believed that our senior citizens in our Jamat were very bored because they weren't enough program to get involved. I always believed to help the sick, deprived, the depressed and I always thought in my mind, "why don't we do something for the seniors as we have for the youths. Mr. Kassamali, the chairman of ISAT, always used to ask me why I don't do something for the seniors. Using my creative mind. I came up with the idea to form a team of youths and seniors together and make them participate in a jeopardy style quiz competition. This was the seniors and the youths can embrace each other and be part of one team. Since this never happened in regular basis in Jamatkhana, using jeopardy style computerized quiz and electronic buzzer system. It was a multi-disciplinary format, they were question on entertainment (name the movie of this video clip), sports, current affairs, Muslim world, Aga Khan Development Network (AKDN), signs, mathematics, current affairs, south east asian (our homeland) and health issues for the seniors. Thus this program was geared to provide knowledge through entertainment to young and old and the entire Jamat. This program was successfully implemented in the following Jamatkhanas (Mosque).

> Headquarters Jamatkhana three times presentation
> Don Mills Jamatkhana two times presentation
> Willowdale Jamatkhana two times presentation
> Etobicoke Jamatkhana two times presentation
> Brampton Jamatkhana one time presentation
> Dundas West one time presentation

This was very successful program and more and more Jamatkhana were requesting for this program but unfortunately, my motor neurons started dying and loosing controls of the muscles and thus I became Palliative and hence cannot continue producing this program. However I want to say that I had lots of fun organizing very creative program under the leadership of previous committee. In fact we used to spend late nights discussing how we can create some program to bring sunshine in the life of our older citizen. Their population as expected to increase dramatically in Canada. I had come up with project proposal but unfortunately I am dying therefore I cannot do justice in its full implementation. This project proposal is very important as it relates to the global financial position and effects the youth's employment, retirement and social life. Please do proper justice in its implementation, here is the project proposal in great detail.

Like Sadrubhai I will be Retiring in the 21st Century what opportunities and challenges awaits me!

- It is early summer morning. The sun has just ambushed the night away and its piercing bright light penetrates through the glass window of my bedroom and interrupts my deep and much needed sleep." Am I late for work"? I burst out. I looked at my clock and calmed down. I was early, how about having breakfast on my patio before heading for work? I thought to myself.

- As I opened the door on this beautiful sunny early morning, and walk down on to my deck, what do I see? My next-door neighbor, the recently retired Sadrubhai, parked in a grey hand knitted hammock mounted on the trunk of two willow trees in his backyard, reading the early morning paper.

- I could feel the aroma of freshly brewed coffee being blown towards me by the early morning breeze, from a coffee percolator on his side.

- Suddenly I see a swarm of birds, mostly oriels and sparrows circling around his deck. I see a huge marble structure near his deck. Astonished as I was, I remembered that must be the much talked about retirement gift from Sadrubhai's employer. A custom made all Italian marble bird feeder with a water fountain directly imported from Italy.

- I could see the birds wetting from the cool fountain water, saluting and thanking Sadrubhai by flapping their wings before flying away into the heaving empty horizon for the rest of the day.

- As my eyes become wide open, what do I see? Sadrubhai's Persian cat "Snowball's newly born five kittens laying on Sadrubhai's chest and messaging his thick white haired chest with their fresh virgin fur. The mother Snowball standing on his side and starring at me as if to give me the message "IF YOU LOVE SOMEONE, SHOW IT".

- Suddenly I hear a voice from Sadrubhai's kitchen. "Sadru have you checked e mail on your new computer about our itinerary for the round the world trip?" Suddenly I see Sadrubhai pick a small gadget from the side table. "That is a Blackberry" I murmured

- To add insult to injury suddenly I spot Sadrubhai's Pompeian puddle dog "Copper" run out of the house to join the party. Copper has been my favorite, usually whenever he sees' me he runs to me and, climbs all over me and never wants to go back. But today he wanted no part of me. He stood by Sadrubhais side with eyes wide open, starring at me as if he never knew me. That was it

■ By now my desire to have a quite long breakfast on the deck had been forgotten due to sudden surge in activity in my neighbor's backyard. My usual cool humanistic nature normally filled with milk of human kindness, had now been overtaken by jealousy, greed and thought of deprivation.

I slammed the patio door shut jumped into my car; Guess what I see in Sadrubhai's driveway. I new brand **35ft Motor home.** This was too much to bear. I closed the door and started driving to work.

■ As I was driving along in the morning rush traffic, thinking about how Sadrubhai's retirement has been magnanimously glorified. What would there be for me when I retire? Would I get an all marble bird feeder? Would I be privileged enough to procure a

Blackberry? Would there be any opportunities for me when I retire, or would my retired life be full of challenges? Let me put it very simply would I be ever able to "retire"? By the time I regained my original composure, well I have reached my office parking lot. Ready for another days work.

Proposal

- The goal is to have a well planned, well organized speech forum for the youths, adults and seniors. They would all be able to express their thoughts on the topic of retirement for the future generations, and what they might expect to face.
- They could also provide suggestions of ways to prepare for the various issues.

Why Choose This Topic?

- The 21st century will be a very unique for retirement as we will have the baby boomers beginning to retire first. These are Ismailis who were educated in the East—migrated to the west, and worked in the west. These will be followed by their children, born in the west. These will be followed by 2nd and 3rd generation Ismailis born and educated in the west.
- The question confronting us will be what opportunities and challenges await these people? And what can we do about it now to prevent some of the hardships that they may encounter?

I am Alysha; I will be retiring in this century. What awaits me? What would make me to retire at 50 and spend week days on the golf Course?

Would I outlive my Baby boomer father, What Health, social, education, Financial CHALLENGES will I face?

Let us brain storm and discuss the issues which will confront us in a speech forum

A Few of Possible Topics . . .

1. Pension

- It seems that there will be enough cash in the Governments coffer for Canada pension and old age pension for the baby boomers, what about for the next group of retirees??
- Currently company's pension plans are in red-deep turmoil (e.g. Automakers, Steel companies etc) will there be any security for company pension for the baby boomers, let alone for the second and third waves of upcoming retirees.
- There is a trend of new employees being hired on contract—or self-employment (no company pension). What will happen when they retire? Would these types of employees be ever able to retire?

- The emphasis here is educated people about starting a Savings Plan at an early age so that they will be ready.

End of retiree medical plan shocks Bell employees
Mar 31, 2007 04:30 AM
JAMES DAW

- Bell Canada employees got a shock this week, but a bigger shock may await them.
- Those who retire within five to 10 years will lose their post-retirement medical benefits once they reach 65. Those who retire later will lose the valuable benefit entirely.
- This is one of the more extreme and uncommon approaches to what has become a common target for cost cutting in Canada, where medical costs are rising and governments are trimming public benefits.

A Few of Possible Topics . . .

2. Health and Life Span

- Almost a quarter of Canadian adults are obese and another third are overweight. This number has risen dramatically since last measured in 1978.
- The situation is equally bleak for Canadian children, where the obesity rate has more than doubled from 3 to 8 percent or 500000 young people. It has also been observed that obese children are prone to liver disease at a very early age.

Obesity shortens kids' life spans: Report

- Mar 27, 2007 03:07 PM
- **CURTIS RUSH**
- STAFF REPORTER the **childhood obesity "epidemic" is so disturbing that today's children will become the first generation in some time to have a shorter life expectancy than their parents, a new report says.**
- **Entitled Healthy Weight for Healthy Kids, the report was issued by the Commons health committee today.**
- The committee said it "shares the fears of many experts who predict that today's children will be the first generation for some time to have poorer health outcomes and a shorter life expectancy than their parents.
- The committee noted that Canada has one of the worst rates of childhood obesity in the developed world.

According to a survey in UK:

- The number of **obese children** has tripled in 20 years. 10% of six year olds are obese, rising to 17% of 15 year olds
- **Obesity is set to become the number one cause of death in UK, according to current trends. Obesity has trebled over the last 20 years and the Health Survey England in 2001 found that around 24 million adults in England are overweight. Of these, 1 in 5 adults are clinically obese and by 2020 this figure is likely to be 1 in 3 according to the Royal College of Physicians.**

What type of life these adults and children have in the 21st century?

Harvard Medical School Report: Loose Weight—Live Longer

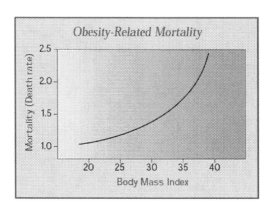

MS—Special Report: Weight Loss (SR96000)

Obesity Trends among Canadian and U.S. Adults, 1985

| No Data ☐ | <10% ▨ | 10%-14% ▨ | 15-19% ▨ | ≥20% ■ |

Obesity Trends among Canadian and U.S. Adults, 2003

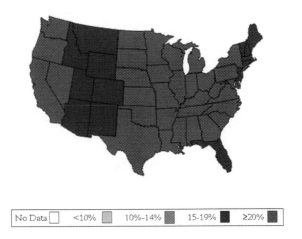

| No Data | <10% | 10%-14% | 15-19% | ≥20% |

We have also noticed that with the medical advances there has been an increase in the life span—or longevity. How will longevity be affected by obesity?

Will obesity reduce the life span?

Or are we geared towards a long unhealthy life span—laden with inactivity and various health problems?
If so, how is it going to affect socially interaction?

Are we going to see Jamatkhanas full of wheelchairs and chairs?

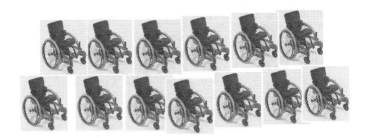

Opportunities & Challenges

- **The secret to happiness, according to researchers, is low expectations. Don't ask for the moon, voyager, when you've got the stars.**
- **Low expectations may trump wealth**
- Apr 01, 2007 04:30 AM
- **LYNDA HURST**
- *"I've been rich and I've been poor. Believe me, rich is better."*
- —Mae West, Gertrude Stein and sundry others
- Yes, well, no argument there. It's better.
- But it's not nirvana.(Ultimate—Absolute—The highest state)
- sssThe age-old assumption that when it comes to money, more equals better, is proving to be just that: an assumption.

3. Volunteerism & Other Opportunities

- Does increase in life span translate increase in voluntary service on retirement, or would there be more burden on the society because of ill health—due to overweight and obesity?
- Due to insecurity in government and company pension means abated voluntary services and "work till you fall apart"?
- Due to increase in life span, would there be opportunities for able bodied retirees to contribute to the jamat and community at large? Will baby boomers be burden, or will they be an important asset as far as globalize volunteering?

- Will there be opportunities for able bodied educated retirees to provide services to various Ismaili institutions overseas?
- Will there ever be Ismaili organizations such as "Doctors or nurses WITHOUT BORDERS"?
- When I was in high school, I vividly remember being taught by a retired teacher from USA, who was part of "Peace Corps" set up by late president John F. Kennedy. Would there be an organization like that for the able bodied retired, educated Ismailis?

Youths work now to retire early?

- According to the 2003 Retirement Confidence Survey by the American Savings Education Council in Washington, D.C., only 21% of saving Americans are very confident of having enough money to live comfortably after they retire. The study also found that three in 10 workers have not saved for retirement.
- **Many Americans retire years before they want to**
- **By Sandra Block and Stephanie Armour, USA TODAY**
- Richard Rocco, 60, of Voorhees, N.J., planned to work as a sales representative until age 65. It hasn't quite worked out that way.
- In January 2005, Rocco's employer, a graphics arts company, downsized and cut his position. Despite 27 years of sales experience, Rocco couldn't find a job. Employers "could get college guys for less than half of what I wanted to work for," he says.
- Rocco, who's single, says he couldn't afford to retire. So he used his 401(k) savings and home equity to buy a PostNet franchise, which provides printing and

graphics services. He enjoys running his own business, but the hours are long. Rocco puts in about 12 hours a day and has yet to draw a salary. He's living off his savings until his business gets off the ground.

- Impact of Education on Retirement in 21st Century—Are our kids going to be on the golf course daily at age 50?
- Or they will be over weight/—victim to obesity and spend lifespan on wheel chairs?????

Overview—The Benefits . . .

- These are few of my thoughts, I am sure jamati will come up with a lot of other original ideas on the opportunities and challenges awaiting them when they retire and provide a holistic thought provoking speech forum.
- This will help in recruiting more members by making them aware of the opportunities in retirement. This will be very appealing to the youths of the jamat.
- This will help in getting more commitment in retirees already involved in volunteering, both badged and unbadged.
- Help the leadership and the council (even the gov't to certain extent) in developing future vision for the retirees.
- Help in enhancing Public speaking skills and enhance the power of oratory for members of all ages. This is especially very important for the youths of our jamat.
- Develop jamats management and leadership skills.
- Provide a networking platform
- Help in developing a sense of empathy for others
- Experience a feeling of achievement

In The Near Future . . .

- If this project is successful in attaining its objectives in GTA, then it could be offered to other provinces and we could host a national Speech forum on Retiring in the 21st Century here in Toronto.
- Details about the logistics of the project such as rules and regulation will be provided later.

For Our Success . . .

- In order to run this program at the highest proficiency level, a trained toastmaster will deliver an hour long presentation on the topic of public speaking, the appropriate content for the main body of the presentation, and finally how to properly conclude a speech.

To help prepare participants for the speech forum, TOASTMASTER is prepared to lead a three hour interactive workshop deal with:

Structure

Central theme or premise that you are passionate about—write a sentence to capture the essence of speech

Opening—capture audience with a startling fact, powerful question, quote, personal story, etc

Body—focus on 3 or 4 well defined points and support with both facts and stories

Conclusion—close on a high with a challenge, a call to action, final thoughts tied back to the beginning.

Content

Anchor to the central theme

Stories and facts to support points

Connect with audience intellectually and emotionally

Make sure the audience has something to walk away with

Delivery

- **Public Speaking Workshop**
- Public Speaking is ranked as the #1 fear for most people even before death. Most people don't like to speak in public because they are afraid of: being ridiculed making a fool of themselves not having anything important to say boring their audience
- The truth is that audiences want speakers to succeed. Speakers can honour their audience's time by being well prepared, animated and authentic and including stories to make a point.
- In order for speakers to have their ideas accepted, they must first work on their non verbal communication. First impressions are very important and lasting. People will buy a product or an idea from another person if they trust in the person delivering the message.
- Speaking in 3D with height, width and depth

- Play attention to energy, vocal variety, eye contact, facial expressions, body gestures, movement, pauses, balance, audience involvement
- Participants will walk away with the fundamentals on how to effectively communicate their ideas.
- The workshop would run approximately 3 hours with a break and several opportunities for audience participation. Feedback would include strengths as well as growth areas for improvement.
- An Adler Trained Professional Coach with a background in Human Resources with a government agency setting. She uses her business savvy in her coaching to help clients get ahead in their careers by conquering their fears and becoming persuasive and effective communicators. She has extensive knowledge and experience in public speaking through Toastmasters and beyond. She has her Distinguished Toastmasters (DTM) status and was named District 60's 2005 'Toastmaster of the Year'.

Branching Out . . .

- **If this project is approved for the entire GTA, various sector divisions can be made as follows:**
- Let us discuss areas such as
- Social effects
- Financial aspects
- Economic impact-
- Would we retire and live in Tajikistan—or other AKF affiliated country?????

Final Goodbye

As I looked through the window at my backyard from a hospital bed, I could see a huge maple tree with the beautiful coloured leaves falling on the ground, still nestled on the top, a few birds nest. I guess all the birds disappeared knowing very soon the leaves will fall and the branches would be all covered with snow and often the trunk is destroyed depending on the severity of the winter. The only thing alive would be the roots or the "brain of the tree". Very similar to my present condition, my body is completely finished, the only thing left is the brain, bone and skin, "even the dog won't eat my bone". My hands, legs, fingers, toes, and feet are all swallowed by ALS tsunami. My muscular right hand which I used to serve with while playing tennis, to baffle the opponent the way Rafael Nadal does in his matches, is today reduced to only bone and skin.

Three years ago this maple tree was only about six inches tall. I used to play in the backyard with my grandson. We used to take turns kicking the softball and then running to pick-it up. But today it is all history in the same way my life would be history, as the following quotes by unknown writers says.

"What will matter are not your memories, but the memories that live in those who loved you.

What will matter is how long you will be remembered, by whom and for what.

What will matter is not your competence, but your character.

What will matter is not how many people you knew, but how many will feel lasting loss when you're gone".

Did I accomplish anything? Was I a good father? Was I good person? The world will have to judge. One thing is for sure I lived a very good life. I enjoyed time my children, my wife, my friends and my parents. I would be doing injustice to my university days if I don't mention the really happy moments I had while being an undergraduate. What comes to my mind are those days, we would go downtown to the movie theater at night and suddenly find out after the movie is over that none of us had anymore change left to pay for the taxi ride to go back to the university. The whole group would set sail on foot, dancing, singing and joking. We would pass by the "Wandagya prostitute's homeland", and would shout and sing loudly to wake them up from whatever they were doing. Sometimes we had to run for our lives. Once we reached our residences at the university we would all gather in one of our friend's room and have coffee, eat something and to also have fun before retiring to bed.

I know I was a very creative person and this creativity I feel was from God but I had the genes of a very creative father. I would be doing injustice if I didn't mention that I was completely immersed with full blessings and a very respectable upbringing from my parents. My father never went to school in India where he was born because at a young age his father died and he had to look after his brothers, sisters and mother. I very vividly remember in our shop in Kyere, Uganda, East Africa, my father would completely dismantle a friend's, customers' bicycles and fix them. I remember when he felt like playing baseball and since they were no baseballs available in our village, he would convert a regular rubber ball into a much harder ball similar to baseball by making a casing of thick fishing net wires around the rubber ball. Thus because of his creativity all the businessman in the village would enjoy a game of baseball.

My dad was an excellent cook not the type that would be cooking in a home kitchen; he would cook very delicious traditional meals for thousands of people on special occasions. I remember on Holy prophet Mohammed's birthday, there used to be special celebration in the Sunni mosque right across our house and my dad would cook delicious Palau (a traditional dish made with rice and meat) for thousands of people. He even cooked the same dish for the president Idi amid dada when he came to visit our town and stopped for prayers at the mosque. Every year in July, we have Imamat Day Celebrations to celebrate the ascension to the throne of Imamat of his highness Karim Aga khan. My father used to be the head cook, cooking for all the Ismaili Muslims living in Sorroti and surroundings. He was so famous that other towns would send a Mercedes to pick him up to cook for them. Thus from my young age doing voluntary service has been a very regular part of my life and I would to like say thanks to my father for this guidance.

My happiest moments

There's still existence in this world of philanthropists like Mr. George Harrison of Mohawk Hospital Services Hamilton, whom I credit for my initial success in Canada. I don't believe that it was by a chance that I met him, but I think it was more than that.

For three days after my daughter had given birth to the first grandchild in our family and the greatest days of my life, I felt I was on the top of the world. But as it goes you can't remain on the top forever. Three days later one of the in laws caused havoc in my house for no reason, and they took away all the glitter, all the sunshine, all the joys from celebration and stressed me out, could this be the cause of my ALS I'm beginning to doubt, could this stressed killed the motor neuron or started killing the motor neuron?

Another happy moment was usually after work on Friday, I would rush home get dressed up for Jamatkhana with my volunteered uniform, rush to pick up by father at the retirement home and go to the Jamatkhana with him. I would parked his wheelchair near me where I was doing my duty. After Jamatkhana services were over, I used to wheel him into the hallway and he used to be swarmed by well wishers and that was very good moment for me and when my mother was still alive my dad would never go to Jamathkhana with her. I wish my mother could see it from upstairs. After Jamatkhana ceremonies the whole family and friends would go to Tim Hortons for a coffee and this old man was with us. He enjoyed his favorite French vanilla and enjoyed the evening before going back to the retirement home.

My trip to Alberta for the National Speech Competition, whereby I took twenty-five trained public speakers from Ontario and represented Ontario extremely well, provided the organizers with proper judging guidelines. This was a great achievement, in fact the respect and the reception we got was tremendous.

I used to take a vacation three times a year and swim in the Atlantic Ocean in Florida together with my family. These memories always stayed with us. We used to have such a great time in Florida. It's like our second home.

I have come up with the very good project proposal titled "Retiring in the twenty first century opportunities and challenges". I hope the leadership carries forward with this project proposal as the events in the globalized world have been changing so fast, that everything narrated in the project proposal is very important. Who knows when there will be a treatment for ALS. I feel it will be very hard to tame this deadly disease, so enjoy as much as you can, don't wait for retirement, enjoy now, now, now. Some of my friends were proud of my disciplined approach to living. For I never used to eat heavy meals after six PM, always went to the gym, played or exercised, never smoked or drank liquor and when they heard that I'm suffering from ALS, they were totally amazed. They thought in their minds that if a disciplined guy like me can get this disease, we definitely can get it too. They immediately booked their vacations, cruises, trips, and etc. to enjoy life.

It was pitch dark night at about 2 am, November 23, 2011. I was in my deep sleep which was very unusual. Usually I'm fighting to get some sleep. Suddenly there was a loud warning whistle from the ventilator. It became dead silent and I started struggling for breath like a non swimmer in the deep end of the swimming pool. The ventilator had stopped pushing air through my lungs due to a power blackout. Suddenly I saw my wife getting up and shaken. She ran and shouted, "The power has gone off." "I have to look for the emergency back-up battery." Luckily she was trained only few days earlier on how to hook-up the emergency back-up battery to the ventilator. Quick action by my wife allowed me to breathe again and I guess to finish the remaining jobs if I have any. Now I know that if God doesn't take me away without torturing me any further then the power supply from Ontario Hydro will definitely do the job. If I had been without any air for another ten minutes I would have gone to my final resting spot. Melvin (Personal Support Worker) came in about nine thirty in the morning. He was totally shocked when he heard about this power failure or outage. He carefully put me on a commode and started our daily routine. I for the first time look at my legs, my God it shocked me, and both my feet have turned black. The feet which used to run five to ten miles and used to take the beating on the tennis courts were today reduced to charcoal. I remember in Africa in my hometown, the butchers didn't have too many walk in coolers to store the slaughtered animals. After hanging the meat for a few days outside it would turn the same color as my feet. He would throw them outside for the wild dogs and other animals to eat. This is how torturous this disease is. Why did I survive the blackout, maybe I'm missing my grandson today to tell him how much I really love him.

One of my darkest moments which totally changed my aspirations and my initial goal in life was my stupidity in not learning Arabic from the mwalimu (the religious imam/teacher) in soroti, Uganda, East Africa in the mosque right across my house. When I was the post-secondary religious education teacher (al-azar) two of my favourite topics were the Glorious Fatimid Period and the other was the "Misperception of Islam in the West". I believe if you look at today's events in the world, these two topics are very pre-dominant in the life of a Muslim living either in the West, Africa or the Middle East currently. I feel Islam needs scholars who believed in global pluralism in order to have peace and tranquility blossom in the world and I BELIEVED THAT I WOULD HAVE MADE A DIFFERENCE.

In all the successes and good relationship I had established with the Toastmasters and its affiliates, setting professional development centers for our community would not have been too far away. This would have invigorated youths and adults to enhance the leadership skills in this competitive globalize meritocratic world. Such a major undertaking requires lots of private supports, teamwork and support from the leadership. I am sure someone would pick this up after I have disappeared from this world, Good luck.

I am just an ordinary men, no Bill Gates nor Steve Jobs but with extraordinary vision for my community and the world at large.

I am writing this book on behalf of the three thousand plus sufferers of ALS in Canada and thousands others worldwide to let the world know that this disease is very treacherous, slow killing and currently incurable, whose cure must be found. I feel ALS society should bring in a paradigan shift in order to get more funding for this disease. Instead of having "walk for ALS" all around the GTA, drawing very small crowds and using up resources unproductively they should learn from organization such as the world partnership walk, (organized by aga khan foundation Canada) or scotiabank run for cancer for successful fund collection achievement.

Last but not the least, I really want to thank my wife in particular, my daughter Alysha, and my grandson Ayaan who has been my inspiration for keeping me going so far and for really taking care of me during this difficult time. Sometimes I have been very irritant, demanding, and very boastful. This is because I have been a very active man throughout my life and being so palliative in such a short time has been very difficult for me, so please forgive me.

I will end with the poem by R. Tagor. It has very deep esoteric meaning and I use it all the time and it is very true.

Go not to the temple to put flowers upon the feet of God,
First fill your own house with the Fragrance of love . . .

Go not to the temple to light candles before the altar of God,
First remove the darkness of sin from your heart . . .

Go not to the temple to bow down your head in prayer,
First learn to bow in humility before your fellowmen . . .

Go not to the temple to pray on bended knees,
First bend down to lift someone who is down-trodden . . .

Go not to the temple to ask for forgiveness for your sins,
First forgive from your heart those who have sinned against you.